30 Ways To Start Manifesting

Jessica McBride

DEDICATION

I'd like to dedicate this book all those in search of their higher self. May this journal guide you toward self-enlightenment, inner peace & ultimately manifesting beyond your wildest dreams.

.

Table of Contents

ACKNOWLEDGMENTS

Dedicated to my ancestors who passed down their gifts to me...I appreciate and honor you for giving me the gift that keeps on giving.
.

1 Cleansing

HUNNY YOU GOTTA SAGE THAT SHIT!!!

When it comes to spirituality and cleansing, most journeys begin with sage. When you burn sage, it generates a thick smoke. That smoke takes the herb from flower to a medicine. This technique is known as Smudging. Sage smoke is like anti-bacterial for energy. It clears out everything negative and positive energy! Once your space is clear and open, anything can enter.

BUT NO WORRIES! You have the power, and this gives you the opportunity to fill the space with the energy that YOU want!

Here are a few steps to sage your space and raise your vibrations:

1. Light your sage.
2. Inhale the smoke and exhale to sage yourself.
3. Make sure to run the smoke through your hair.
4. Start from back of the house/room to the front to push the energy out of a window or a door.
5. Make sure you get the smoke in the corners of the room, behind doors and closets.
6. Choose an incense to burn or an essential oil to diffuse (this is the energy you choose to fill your space with)

Journal intentions for the day now that your space is clear, and energy is raised

_____
_____
_____
_____
_____
_____
_____
_____
_____
_____
_____
_____
_____
_____
_____
_____
_____
_____
_____
_____
_____
_____
_____
_____
_____
_____
_____
_____
_____
_____
_____
_____
_____
_____
_____
_____

30 WAYS TO START MANIFESTING

_____
_____
_____
_____
_____
_____
_____
_____
_____
_____
_____
_____
_____
_____
_____
_____
_____
_____
_____
_____
_____
_____
_____
_____

2 Create Your Sacred Space

Everyone has a God or Goddess within & deserves a space they can call their own to pray, meditate, or just focus your energy to stay centered so you can manifest or release whatever you need from within! Only you can define what sacred means to you; this space can be as big as a room or a closet or as simple as a special shelf or table within a room.

Here are steps to create a sacred space:
- Add items that you love or hold special value: Items that reflect your spiritual beliefs, or symbols that bring positivity to you (example, Christian cross, Buddha statue, pictures of saints or deities)
- Pictures of your ancestors, close relatives or loved ones
- Balance the elements:
  Air: Incents & incent holders or essential oil diffuser
  Water: Find a nice cup or bowl and add water
  Fire: Candles
  Earth: Store your sage here, but also add your favorite crystals, stones or herbs

- Positive Affirmations:

Write 3- 5 affirmations that you will say daily to feed positivity to your soul Example: "I am full of love and light!"

My Affirmations:
1._____

_____

_____

2._____

_____

_____

3._____

_____

_____

4._____

_____

_____

5._____

_____

_____

_____

_____

_____

Journal your thoughts afterwards.

_____

_____

_____

_____

_____

_____

_____

_____

_____

_____
_____
_____
_____
_____
_____
_____
_____
_____
_____
_____
_____
_____

3 Sunday- Sun

The Sun is associated with abundance!

Sunday Associations:
- Fire element
- Cleansing
- Hope for the Future
- Victory & Success
- Family
- Blessing
- New Beginnings
- Zodiac Signs: Leo, Aries, Sagittarius

The Sun shines light and gives life! It's the day that we give thanks for what we already have and what we are about to receive. In order to receive we must first cleanse our spirit so there are no areas where your light can't shine. Write a short letter forgiving someone, or yourself most importantly. This is the start of your journey to abundance!

_____

_____

_____
_____
_____
_____
_____
_____
_____
_____
_____
_____
_____
_____
_____
_____
_____
_____
_____
_____
_____

4 Releasing: Dark Moon Ritual

The Dark Moon is the Moon phase when you cannot see the moon in the sky. Download the Moon Phase App, when it says the "new moon" is at 0% that is the dark moon phase. The Dark moon phase is in conjunction & right before the New Moon. It is when the moon is directly between the earth and the sun. When the sky is dark, there is void of light, and it makes a great time to release or empty yourself of what does not serve you before you start to take steps to manifest what you want to bring into your life!

Do you ever have problems, letting things go? Here is a quick technique to use in the physical world to get out of your head and move forward manifesting what you want out of life!

Be honest with yourself that you are ready to let go of that person, place, thing or bad habit!

- On top of your journal paper write, "I (insert name) release…"
- List everything you want to let go. (i.e., fear, bad eating habits, my ex, etc.)

- Read it out loud.

- Scratch out each item you said you wanted to let go until you can't see what you wrote anymore.
- State out loud: "I release these things from my life, and shall I said it, so it be done!
- Light the paper on fire until it turns completely to ashes (do this outside or burn in metal tray, or trash can)
- Once the pile is ashes, blow it away from you

------------------------------CUT HERE------------------------------

I REALEASE (LIST 3 THINGS):

_____

I'M LETTING GO OF (LIST 3 THINGS):

_____

I WILL STOP (LIST 3 THINGS):

_____
I RELEASE THESE THINGS FROM MY LIFE, AND
SHALL I SAID IT, SO IT BE DONE!

_____
_____
_____
_____
_____
_____
_____
_____
_____
_____

_____
_____
_____
_____
_____
_____
_____
_____
_____
_____
_____

.

JESSICA MCBRIDE

.

5 Monday – Moon

Monday is the day of the moon, the moon controls our emotions.

Day Associations:
- Water Element
- Dreams
- Healing
- Windows & Doors
- Career & Work
- Study & Meditation
- Water Signs: Pisces, Cancer, Scorpio
- Air Signs: Aquarius, Gemini, Libra

Moon is all about your inner emotions. Take the time to reflect on the past week and how you felt about it. Now write about how you can utilize the Moon energy to connect closer to yourself, your dreams, goals, and wishes for this upcoming week. What things are you closing out and walking towards? Focus on what feels right. Follow your heart & not your head!

_____
_____
_____

JESSICA MCBRIDE

_____
_____
_____
_____
_____
_____
_____
_____
_____
_____
_____
_____
_____
_____
_____
_____
_____

6 New Moon Ritual

Time for new beginnings that is what the new moon is all about!
Many people take this time to start manifesting but wonder why
their dreams, wishes goals aren't coming to fruition. So, make
sure that you do the releasing ritual first. You use the New
Moon energy to help you begin things, plant a seed or take the
first step towards what you want to manifest.

Journal about what you want to give new life to and bring into
your life:

(Use phrases such as I'd like to start, I'd like to begin, I want to
bring ____ into my life)

_____
_____
_____
_____
_____
_____
_____
_____
_____
_____
_____

JESSICA MCBRIDE

_____
_____
_____
_____
_____
_____
_____
_____
_____
_____
_____

7 Cold Bath

If things are feeling a little out of whack, a Cold wash is a great way to get clear any blockages and raise your vibrations! Add the following ingredients into a large pot and sit it in the refrigerator for 30 minutes. Get undressed and go kneel in the bath tub. Tilt your head down & pour the water over the back of your neck. Let the water & the herb run down your body. Then be still, meditate and simply FEEL!

- Coconut water
- Coconut milk
  Lavender
- Jasmine
- Rosemary
- Fill the rest with water

Write down how you felt, what you let wash away & what thoughts came to mind as you were meditating:

_____
_____
_____
_____

JESSICA MCBRIDE

_____
_____
_____
_____
_____
_____
_____
_____
_____
_____
_____
_____
_____
_____
_____
_____
_____
_____
_____
—

8 Manifesting

Time to bring what you deserve to you, but how? You need to write down what you want, but how do you want to get it, and when do you want it. Sometimes we cast a huge net over the blessings the universe has in store for us, but we end up only catching a small part of what we want, and not exactly how you wanted. It's because you need to be more specific. Utilize the SMART goal model.

Example: I'd like to manifest a $100 to me from getting a bonus at my job by the end of the month!
Credit: Karthost.com

JESSICA MCBRIDE

9 Meditation 101

Focus on how you want your day to be. Create a self-affirmation!

(Example: I am a magnet for miracles!)

_____

_____

_____

_____

Go to your sacred space: Refer to "Making your space sacred", and follow those steps.

The frequency of sound effects thinking, so depending on how you focus, put on music that resonates with your spirit, or sit in silence.

Sit with your knees crossed below your hips, so you may need to sit on pillows or laydown.

Close eyes and start breathing in for 4 seconds, hold for 4 seconds, release for 4 seconds.

You can't always "quiet" your thoughts. Imagine a bookshelf in your mind, so as thoughts come in your head, listen to them and

shelf the idea. Do not try to solve it or fix it. Write down your
daily meditations

_____
_____
_____
_____
_____
_____
_____
_____
_____
_____
_____
_____
_____
_____
_____
_____
_____
_____
_____
_____
_____

10 Healing Bath

Feeling like life is against you? You may be crossed or jinxed by yourself or others. Here are the steps to shock your system and take the 1st step towards healing yourself!

Get 4 candles and place them in each corner of the tub. This makes your space sacred and creates a "wall" of protection around you.

- Black candle – Absorb negative energy

- White candle – To cleanse and connect you closer to your God aka Higher Self

- Red candle – Emotional strength and protection

- Blue candle – Healing

1.Run warm bath water.

2. Add the following ingredients to the bath water: (most found in your kitchen).

- Pink Himalayan sea salt

- 1 tbsp. of apple cider vinegar
- 4 oz. of Rosemary
- 4 oz. of Basil

3. Get in the tub and focus on the candle lights as you calm your mind and start to meditate.

Submerge your entire body under the water to your ears, leaving your eyes, mouth, and nose outside the water – 10 minutes.

Listen to your heartbeat and focus on the messages that pop into your mind.

Pat dry once you get out of the tub, and let the herbs naturally fall off of you.

Write down the messages that came to you while you were under water.

_____
_____
_____
_____
_____
_____
_____
_____
_____
_____
_____
_____
_____
_____
_____
_____
_____
_____
_____
_____

11 Grounding Yourself

Feeling a little out of touch with reality, time to ground yourself! This one is easy.

1.Go outside and find grass and a tree.

2.Take off your shoes and socks and step on the grass barefoot.

3.Put your right hand on the tree.

4.Close your eyes

5.Walk clockwise around the tree 3 times while inhaling and exhaling.

6.Take a seat under the tree with your back touching the tree Enjoy nature!!! Feel free to people watch, enjoy the breeze and feel free to journal your dreams, goals, and wishes.

Journal Your Experiences

_____
_____
_____
_____
_____
_____
_____
_____
_____

12 Cord Cutting

Got a toxic ex or friend? Can't get them out of your head? That's because you are connected. No matter if the situation ended on good terms or not, you created a bond with someone that isn't easy to break, even after a breakup. Are you ready to get rid of a certain someone? Time to cut cords! Here is how to do it!

1.Take a picture of yourself and the other person. Write on the back of the person you want to let go picture the following:

- Their name and birthday
- "I forgive you for."
- Write what they did to hurt you
- Their name again
- "I release you from my life."
- Write on the back of your picture the following:
- Your name and birthday
- "I forgive myself for."
- Write down a small note to yourself forgiving yourself for your part in the situation.

Take a piece of rope and tie it to your picture and the other person's picture with a few inches of slack in between

Say the following: "I cut these cords that have bound us."

Take a pair of scissors and cut the cord between the 2 pictures.

On the section with your ex's picture, take a lighter and burn their piece of the cord and picture

Make sure it burns all the way and throw that part in the trash

POOF BE GONE!!!

Use the space below to write out why you are ready to cut cords with this person.

_____
_____
_____
_____
_____
_____
_____
_____
_____
_____
_____
_____
_____
_____
_____
_____
_____
_____
_____
_____
_____
_____
_____

13 My Goals

Goals are essential to manifesting. They are realistic to physical world & can be achieved within a reasonable amount of time.

"Refer to Manifesting 101"

People tend to get overwhelmed because they set huge blanket goals that are long term, and only focus on the BIG WINS. It takes a lot of small victories to get to a big one.

Write down 5 short term goals you want to accomplish over the next 30 days:

_____
_____
_____
_____
_____
_____
_____
_____
_____
_____
_____

14 My Wishes

Wishes are essential to manifesting. They are the things that are realistic to the physical world yet may not seem achievable in a reasonable amount of time. It can be either something you want immediately or that you think would take a long time to come to fruition.

Be sure to be careful what you wish for, because you will get it. Be truthful to yourself and don't cut yourself short. Once a wish comes true you are going to wish you asked the universe for more!

Write down your wishes:

_____
_____
_____
_____
_____
_____
_____
_____
_____
_____

JESSICA MCBRIDE

.

15 My Dreams

Dreams are essential to manifesting. They are the things that are not realistic to the physical world. In fact, they are out of this world!!!

As we get older, our dreams get smaller. Go back to when you were a kid and dream like the inner child that lives within you!

You never know what the universe has in store for you!
DREAM BIG!!!

_____
_____
_____
_____
_____
_____
_____
_____
_____
_____
_____
_____
_____

JESSICA MCBRIDE

16 Tuesday- Mars

Tuesday is the day of Mars. Mars is known for being associated with war.

Day Associations:
- Fire Element
- Divine Masculine Energy
- Protection
- War
- Strength in the mind and body
- Confidence
- Loyalty – Friendship, Relationships/Marriage, Business Partnerships
- Purging through Fire
- Sexual Encounters
- Fire Signs: Aries, Leo, Sagittarius

Mars is the planet of war but not just fighting an enemy, but more about taking action and "going to war" for yourself, going for what you want. When warriors go to war, they are uniting behind one mission they have unwavering faith for. This is usually someone else's dream or goal that they believe in. Time to believe in your mission more than anything in the world! What is it that you need to foster inner strength, confidence, AKA the energy of Mars to progress forward for YOU?

.

17 Protection

We all need to protect ourselves, and here is one way to go about it. You can protect yourself physically, mentally, emotionally or spiritually.

We are going to cover all those areas generally. This would be good to do on Tuesday, the day of Mars!

- The black candle absorbs negative energy & spiritual protection
- The red candle is for emotional protection & strength
- The Green candle is for mental protection & healing
- The brown candle is for physical protection & grounding

Set the candles in a circle.

Take salt and use it to connect each candle in a circular pattern

You can choose to put yourself in the center, or a symbol of who/what you want to protect yourself from in the center.

(Remember that what is placed in the center is protected, but it cannot get out either, so make sure you set your intentions

specifically and choose if you need to create a barrier around yourself or bind something from yourself or the world.)
Light the candles.

Speak your intentions into each flame

Let the universe do the rest.

Write about the situation you need protection from.

_____
_____
_____
_____
_____
_____
_____
_____
_____
_____
_____
_____
_____
_____
_____
_____
_____
_____
_____
_____
_____
_____
_____
_____

_____
_____
_____
_____
_____
_____
_____
_____
_____
_____
_____
_____

18 Wednesday- Mecury

Wednesday is the day of Mercury. Mercury is the planet of communication.

Day Associations:

- Air Element
- Water Element
- Movement
- Communication – Actual verbal communication between people.
- Technology - Devices we use to send and receive messages.
- Transportation
- Dancing

Mercury is all centered on the flow of energy, ideas, and messages. Moving as free as the air and flowing as smooth as water. It's time to write a letter to your future self. Send yourself a message of gratitude and congratulations for achieving the goal or the manifestations you want to come to fruition. This will help you move your intentions forward to reveal them in the physical world!

_____

_____

JESSICA MCBRIDE

19 Open Your Third Eye

Everyone can connect to his or her third eye. The third eye related directly to the Anja chakra. The one in between your eyebrows. The third eye leads you to your high-self and spiritual realm. The third eye is our ability to see what might be, to see potential.

Here is the formula to a paste you can make and use when you meditate to help activate and open your 3rd eye.

- 1-part sea salt
- 1/2 Ricketts Crown Blue Square
- 25 drops of Oracle Oil
- 20 drops of Patchouli
- A teaspoon of Eyebright Powder

Stir together until it turns a paste

Add water if needed to gain consistency

Put a circle of the paste on your 3rd eye area

Go to your sacred space

Start your meditation process

Write down messages received during mediation

_____
_____
_____
_____
_____
_____
_____
_____
_____
_____
_____
_____
_____
_____
_____
_____
_____
_____
_____
_____
_____
_____
_____
_____

20 Thursday - Jupiter

Thursday is the day of Jupiter. Jupiter is the planet of luck & success.

Day Association:

- Earth Element
- Grounding
- Success
- Business
- Finances
- Legal matters
- Control, Power & Domination
- Reaping Harvest
- Earth Signs: Capricorn, Taurus, Virgo

Jupiter is the largest planet in our solar system. It holds a lot of power to take on a lot and move things in your favor. This is a great time to channel the 3 C's: Control, Compel, & Command to bring success to you. Whether its business success, money or achieving a goal write down your action plan to achieve your large WIN!! Be Specific and write down what you want, when you want it, who you are working with, why, and how you plan to succeed! Then go and take action!

21 Money Maker

Manifesting Money is very common. Here is a simple charm
to make which will bring money to your wallet. First,
remember always to do this in your sacred space, & cleanse
your area! Do your money manifestation work on a Thursday,
the day of Jupiter, financial success!

Take a green glass candle and clean it with Florida Water
On the bottom write in permanent marker "stable economic
foundation."

Then from the bottom up write the following:

- Full Name
- Birthday
- Phrases about bringing money to you

Examples:
- Manifesting money
- Bring devoted clients
- Fast money
- Business success
- Close new business deals
- $1,000 in my account

Sprinkle mint, basil, and allspice into the top of the candle.

Leave a little space around the wick

Light the candle
Speak what you want to bring to you into the flame.

Pick a real dollar bill... you pick the amount. I usually pick a $2 bill or $20.

Write on the back of the dollar bill your name and the front the phrase, "MANIFESTING MONEY."

Roll the dollar bill towards you, to bring money towards you, and have you "rolling in dough."

Once you have melted candle wax. Dip the rolled bill into the candle wax, be careful of the flame.

Unroll the bill and rub the wax over the entire bill
Repeat the dipping process until the entire bill is covered in wax
Place the money charm in your wallet, and do not spend it!
Once your candle burns out, place it in your sacred space
 Continue to add things to the empty candle such as coins, dollars, money herbs, money oils, money draw crystals.

Write your money manifesting phrases below that you will put on your candle.

_____
_____
_____
_____
_____
_____
_____
_____
_____
_____
_____
_____
_____
_____

30 WAYS TO START MANIFESTING

JESSICA MCBRIDE

_____
_____
_____
_____
_____
_____

22 Prosperity Pumpkin

This is a great ritual to do during the fall equinox! Or on a Thursday or Sunday! The pumpkin symbolizes a womb or a place to incubate and grow what you want to bring your way. This is all about gathering your resources and creating a path for abundance.

Follow these steps:

1. Pick a pumpkin that you connect with, not too small, but not crazy big.
2. Cleanse the pumpkin with Florida water.
3. Cut a circle around the top of the pumpkin and remove the top.
4. Take a spoon and gut all the insides out of the pumpkin. (This process represents the hard work you will put in to reap what you sow.)

5. Take the guts and remove the seeds, set seeds to the side
6. Write a petition about what you want to bring to you
7. Fold petition towards you and stick it in the middle of the pumpkin.
8. Start to fill the pumpkin with prosperity herbs: (you do not have to use all, just use the herbs that resonate with you)
a. Cinnamon

b. All Spice
c. Mints
d. Basil
e. Bergamot
f. Chamomile
g. Clover
h. Lemon Verbena

9. Fill the herbs with crystals that resonate with you: Ex: Jade, laborite, garnet, citrine.
10. Take symbols from your job, businesses & passions. For example business cards, pictures) cut them into small pieces and sprinkle them within the pumpkin.

11. You may also fill the pumpkin with the following: think vision board inside the pumpkin.

• Money
• Coins
• Cut up pictures of places you'd like to visit.
• Pictures of friends, family and loves ones.

12. Cover the fillings with honey
13. Take good luck or prosperity incense and stick 3 inside the pumpkin in a triangle formation.
14. Light the incense.
15. Meditate with the incense smoke, as they burn all the way out.
16. Close the pumpkin.
17. Take a yellow tapered candle & light it.
18. Let the candle wax drip in a clockwise motion over the crease in the pumpkin top to seal it.
19. Let the pumpkin sit in your scared space area until the next New Moon.
20. Take the pumpkin to the river or any area with flowing water and release the pumpkin into the water.

Write your Prosperity Pumpkin Petition below:

23 Friday- Venus

Friday is the day of Venus. Venus is the planet of relationships & collaborations.

Day Associations:
- Water Element
- Air Element
- Earth Element
- Love/Passion
- Sexuality, Seduction & Sensuality
- Beauty
- Friendship
- Gathering of People: Parties, Vacations & Dates
- Planting Seeds; Fruitfulness
- Reconciliation
- Zodiac signs – Libra & Taurus

Venus is a planet that sends out and receives loves. Unlike the moon that deals with your inner emotions, Venus deals with how you project love out to the world and reaping what you have sewed. Time to claim what you deserve! Write down 3-5 affirmations about loving yourself. Plant the seeds and watch them bloom!

_____
_____
_____
_____
_____
_____
_____
_____
_____
_____
_____
_____
_____
_____
_____
_____
_____
_____
_____

24 Self-Love - Rosewater

We can all use a boost of self-love from time to time. Here is a great project to literally pour love into yourself!

Go to your favorite store and purchase a bouquet of pink roses

Get a 375ml bottle of Ever clear

Pour half of the liquid into a separate bowl or cup

Pick each petal of the rose stem into a bowl (while picking think about all the things you love about yourself

Once you have your bowl of rose petals, swirl the bowl around clockwise and say, "I am made of love & light!" – 7 times

Insert each petal into the half-full bottle of Ever clear

Take a funnel and pour the rest of the Ever clear into the bottle filled with roses until the bottle is full

Close bottle tight and keep in the medicine cabinet for 2 weeks

Every morning and/or night when you brush your teeth or shower pull out the bottle and shake it while smiling in the mirror and telling yourself, "I am made of love & light!"

After 2 weeks, take a spray bottle, insert a funnel and hold the strainer over the funnel, pour out Ever clear bottle with roses

Close bottle, and BOOM Healing Rosewater you can spray on yourself!

Write a love letter to yourself.

_____
_____
_____
_____
_____
_____
_____
_____
_____
_____
_____
_____
_____
_____
_____
_____
_____
_____
_____
_____
_____
_____
_____
_____
_____

25 Sacred Dancing

Merging Divine Feminine & Divine Masculine energy inside
your sacral chakra area is powerful. Sexual energy is sacred &
can channel healing into your vital organs and increase
emotional, physical, mental and spiritual health! The sacred
sacral dance is used to move that energy from deep within
you, unblock any barriers within you and help you manifest.
Go to your sacred space. Cleanse the energy and turn on music
that resonates with your Divine Feminine or Divine Masculine
energy. Then DANCE!!!! Your dance may start off small &
sweet, but as the song plays, open up and let go. Literally
dance like no one is watching! Journal how you feel after,
below!

_____

_____

_____

_____

_____

_____

_____

_____

_____

_____

JESSICA MCBRIDE

84

_____
_____
_____
_____
_____
_____
_____
_____
_____
_____
_____

26 My Ideal Partner

Prepare yourself to receive love. People talk down on "the list." This is the list people make of things they expect their partner to have in order to choose them.

I say to hell with those people. Just as much as we can manifest what we want in a job or home, you can manifest what you want in a partner!

Take the time to make your wish list, if you could create your ideal partner in a test tube, what he/she would look like, act like, where have they been, what are they doing now and where are they going in the future.

This would be great to do under the Full Moon energy or on a Friday, the day of Venus!

_____
_____
_____
_____
_____
_____
_____
_____
_____
_____

-

_____
_____
_____
_____
_____
_____
_____
_____
_____
_____
_____
_____
_____
_____

27 Saturday- Saturn

Saturday is the day of Saturn. Saturn is associated with discipline.

Day Associations:
* Earth Element
* Letting go of old habits
* Releasing
* Personal Routines & Self-care
* Mental Stability
* Liberation & Freedom
* Brainstorming & New ideas
* Zodiac sign Capricorn

Saturn is all about getting things done, the right way! This is a good day to reflect on the past week and determine where we could do better. We work so hard for others during the week; this day is all about taking time out for yourself. Create a plan for a self-care routine to help you get serious about improving YOU moving forward. (Example: I will drink a gallon of water every day, I will give myself a facial once a week, I will work on my personal business plan for 1 hour every day.)

_____

_____

JESSICA MCBRIDE

28 Truth Tub

Great to do on a Saturday

1.   This bath you can do alone with a mirror, or with a lover.

2.   Add the following to the tub: This floral blend cleanses, supports emotional healing & helps release negativity of the past.

- Sea Salt
- Rosemary
- Lavender
- Hibiscus
- Calendula
- Pink Rose

3.   Declare this area a safe space, free of judgment and what is said here will stay here.

4.   Sit in the tub with a hand mirror or a standing mirror you can place in the water OR sit in the tub with your partner face to face.

JESSICA MCBRIDE

5.   Take turns telling each other the truth, things you may have been scared to say to each other, or ask each other questions?
6.   In this tub is where we listen and receive the messages that come to us and forgive.

7.   Then talk about how you are going to move forward together.

8.   Once you are done talking with yourself, or your partner.

9.   Let the water out and let those things you need to let go wash down the drain.

Write down what truths came from the tub, how it made you feel, and how you will move forward knowing this truth.

_____

94

When the moon is full it has reached its ultimate potential & it has nothing left to do but to release itself. Do the same thing for yourself. Give thanks for all the hard work you have put in & what you have achieved. Then, take the time to let go of the negativity. Utilize the chart below to guide you on areas of your life to manifest and create full moon rituals around those topics.

Month	Moon	Ritual Suggestion
January	Wolf Moon	Gathering your tribe, or pack, ask to increase your bond and protection
February	Snow Moon	Connect with your ancestors to help guide your future
March	Worm Moon	Sow your desires
April	Pink Moon	Reap what you sowed, give thanks & gratitude for what's

		coming to you
May	Flower Moon	Rethink, reevaluate and restate your goals
June	Strawberry Moon	Balance your lower-self (primal needs & desires) & your higher-self (spiritual needs & desires)
July	Buck Moon	Plan next steps after you receive your manifestation. Now What?
August	Sturgeon Moon	Push through adversity, or swim against the current
September	Corn Moon	Gather your resources, utilize all elements of air, fire, earth & water
October	Blood Moon	Release yourself of low vibrating energy & negative thoughts
November	Snow Moon	Give thanks for what you have received and your tribe around you
December	Oak Moon	Access how far you have come and where you want to go moving forward

_____
_____
_____
_____
_____
_____
_____
_____

_____
_____
_____
_____
_____
_____
_____
_____
_____
_____
_____
_____

30 Blue Moon Ritual

A blue moon is when more than 1 full moon happens within the same month. This happens once every 2-3 years. Blue moons are perfect times to make special wishes about your dreams, things that wouldn't happen every day! Here are some easy steps:

- Take the time to make a wish, write it down with your name.

- Tear this page

- Put it outside under the blue moonlight, putting this paper over grass or partially in dirt is even better.

- Let it sit over-night

- Next morning take it out and let dry if needed in the sunlight.

- Place paper under your mattress where you lay your head.

Let the universe do the rest.

JESSICA MCBRIDE

ABOUT THE AUTHOR

Jessica McBride is a Manifestationalist and Happiness
Catalyst. I serve the spiritual community healing and
supporting those who need help intentionally manifesting
for their highest good. I have an intentional tea blend
businesses, called Manifest Tea, where I create
decadent, holistic, intentionally blended herbal teas to be
integrated into your manifestation routine. I am a
herbalist, tarot reader, and Hounsi Bonswal.. AKA self-
proclaimed wild spiritual woman. I utilize a blend of
catholic symbolism, African & native based spirits, my
direct ancestors, and nature to perform my healing work
for the world.

Made in the USA
Middletown, DE
07 February 2023

24213739R00066